Thoughts on Life

by

Fiona Halliday

First published 2024 by The Hedgehog Poetry Press,

5 Coppack House, Churchill Avenue, Clevedon. BS21 6QW

www.hedgehogpress.co.uk

ISBN: 978-1-916830-41-7

Cover design © Liz Stirk

Contents

To my family, thank you for all your support.

WHAT DO YOU THINK?

What do you think
Of the trash-choked oceans
And the dying creatures?

What do you think
Of the cash-starved NHS
And the exhausted workers being exploited?

What do you think
Of refugees being sent to other continents
And the desperation of families?

What do you think
Of the rise in prices
And the poverty of children?

What do you think
Of the state of our climate
And the loss of many bees?

What do you think
Of the lack of compassion
And love for humankind?

What should we think?

PROTECT THE EARTH

Above us, clouds form,
Below us, worms wriggle,
How we must protect the Earth.
Beside us, animals live,
Feeding us, plants grow,
How we must protect the Earth.
Enabling us, bees work,
Quenching thirst, rains fall,
How we must protect the Earth.
We must act now,
We must take care,
We must protect the Earth.

TIGER

Tiger
Stripes, teeth and roar
Stealthy hunter, stalks prey
Unmerciful, but beautiful
Purring.

CHRYSANTHEMUM

He arrived on her doorstep,
A bunch of red roses in hand,
Roses, and one, yellow chrysanthemum.

What did the chrysanthemum denote?
An emblem of innocence lost?
An apology for betrayal?
Perhaps, it was to lessen the romance, the ardour of the roses?
Maybe, it was to remind her of her youthfulness?
Did its presence make her laugh her tinkling giggle?
Did it make her run to him?

No.
She stood at the open doorway,
Eyes direct with maturity and self-respect.
She half-smiled at the flowers,
She understood.
Silently, she made her choice,
Slowly, gracefully, she closed the door.
She went back into her home,
Her own self intact.

IS THIS A LOVE POEM?

Looking at you from across the room,
Remembering how it all began,
A group of friends in common,
A spilled drink and lots of laughs.
Twenty plus years of laughter and love,
Losing patience and parenting,
Losing parents and payslips,
Holding our time together with
Sticky tape and stickier fingers.
Is this a love poem?
Looking at you from across the hall,
Remembering that first Valentine card,
You still "make my heart smile like the sun",
For every misplaced word and set of keys,
There are a hundred memories,
Mundane and momentous,
Fortunate and fragile,
Our lives entwined like lovers,
Our love entwined throughout our lives.
Is this a love poem?
Love seeping into every occasion,
Good or bad,
You are still my only one,
I am still your love,
Thank you for all the little things,
I'm grateful for the great times,
And trust for all the difficult ones.
Is this love essential?
Yes, yes, yes!
Is this a love poem?

MAY WE REMEMBER

How short our memories are,
One moment wishing to say, "thank you",
Next, annoyed as traffic is stopped
By the bin collection lorry.
How short our memories are,
Promises made that NHS staff will be
Properly paid,
Clapping did not give them money for electricity.
How short our memories are,
A long time locked into our homes,
Conversing over the internet,
Missing loved ones.
Now, there is impatience on the roads,
People shout in the streets,
Anger, a lack of compassion and kindness.
How short our memories are,
Once, we recognised the cleanliness of the air,
The sound of birds,
Seeing mountains and clear, azure skies.
But still the virus rages on,
Now we are to 'live with it.'

Deaths are still happening,
But they are no longer newsworthy,
How short our memories are.

REGRET

Rain-bright grass
Glistens, reminding
Of carefree days.
Cloud-soft skies
Pretend innocent days
Are still here.
Guilt-darkened thoughts
Invade the mind
Taking peace.
Sun-warmth gives hope
Of forgiveness.

SLEEP

Finding the way to sleep,
Through a maze of memories,
Thoughts turn like mobiles in the wind,
Ideas chime and peal their laughter,
Excited about what lies ahead.
Finding the way to sleep,
Through a haze of heaviness,
Worries roll around like waves crashing on the shore,
Regrets whisper and repeat their menace,
Confusing the mind about what lies in the past.

Finding the way to sleep,
Sometimes, it is not easy,
But when sleep arrives,
It provides respite and relief.
In the morning, some difficulties may seem smaller,
Those that don't, will hopefully,
be met with better strength.

LET'S LIVE

Let's pour delight from cups of bright sunlight
Let's gather happiness as a hen gathers chicks
Let's see the goodness in people around us
Let's pick positivity from a bundle of sticks.

Let's feed imaginations from a world of daydreams
Let's give generosity wrapped up like a gift
Let's look for a way forward with gentleness and safety
Let's pluck strings of joy, feel our spirits lift.

Let's remember with love those who've gone before us
Let's keep making memories with hopeful hearts
Let's share our knowledge and compassion
Let's show forgiveness is where love starts.

Let's teach our children to be who they are
Let's teach ourselves to take time to rest
Let's pour delight from cups of bright sunlight
For life is uncharted, let's keep our zest!

PRAYER FOR PEACE

On this day
We hear news
Of war and death
We pray for peace.

On this day
We see reports
Of families killed
We pray for peace.

On this day
We read stories
Of people fleeing
We pray for peace.

Lord, this injustice, this terror
Threatens our whole world's way of being
Crying out for others
We pray for peace.

WARTIME

During times of war...
Our words are so small,
People desperately trying to survive,
To look after their young,
To shelter the elderly,
They're fighting each day to stay alive.
These are not people far removed,
They are families like yours or mine,
Whatever the country,
Whatever the situation,
We see the futility,
We witness the desolation,
We fear,
Fear is all around us.
The world has got smaller,
Our words are inadequate.

(This poem can be read from top to bottom, and then bottom to top.)

HOPE AND FRIENDSHIP

My wish for you is a long table
Filled with food
Surrounded by loved ones
My hope for you is a long life
Filled with happiness
Accompanied by joyful memories
My thoughts of you are of a long friendship
Filled with laughter
Supported by companionship.

MISSING YOU

Grief grasps my heart with vicelike grip
At Christmas, on Birthdays and Anniversaries,
On the day, I am usually fine,
Distracted by other family members,
Your grandchildren are growing up,
They have your love of music and drama,
And are much sportier than me or their dad.
It's in the quieter moments, it hits again,
the wave.
I watched a programme about guitars today,
You'd have enjoyed it,
You'd have made them sing, and people laugh.
You are never forgotten,
But you are missed, every day,
Thank you for your legacy.

JOURNEY

Journeying through life,
Watching people come and go,
Some leave peacefully,
Many walk difficult paths,
May your steps be calm and blessed.

FEAR

The fear of silence
In a full room, the fear of
Speaking, out of turn.

LIGHT

Darkness dispelled by the smallest light,
Sight given with a single candle,
Frost melted by a lit match,
Hope felt in the dead of night.

Stars burn light years away,
The moon borrows her glimmer,
Shadows fall, proving the strength,
Of the winter's sun.

Electric illumination to banish fears,
Dreams filled with laughter,
Dancing flames from crackling fires,
Celebrate warmth and fellowship.

OUTSIDE, LOOKING IN

When I'm outside, looking in,
I feel alone, angry, scared,
Your silence, like the birds before a storm,
Haunts me.
I'm outside your mind, your thoughts closed,
Just like your lips and clenched fists,
Unwilling, unable to articulate,
Your fears.
Each time, I hope, pray that the darkness
Will pass, and we will share the bright morning.

TIME RAN OUT

The time ran out
The time to laugh and sing
The time to be held
The time to be reminded
You are loved.

The time ran out
The time to work and think
The time to be heard
The time to say we're sorry
You are loved.

The time ran out
The time to learn and speak
The time to be happy
The time to spend with your family
You are loved.

Inside eternity
Outside of our time
You are loved.

REMEMBERING

An infectious giggle and a twinkle in the eye,
Beautiful and brave, you spoke your mind,
We loved to hear stories of your exploits,
Adventures with cousins, auntie, dad,
Tandem cycling (or not),
Ice creams and banana milkshakes,
Your summers sounded idyllic.
Memories of games played in the garden,
Charades and shenanigans,
You will be missed.
You are gone from our sight, but not forgotten,
You had a passion for angels and Elvis,
And the stars overhead,
Your children and family, wonderful memories,
You are loved, now and always.

CATS

Cats stare,
Seemingly into the soul,
Their green lights illuminating,
The darkest heart.
Cats stare,
But as they blink,
They show their love,
Contentment in a purr,
Intention to sleep.
Do not fear a cat's stare,
They see the soul,
And accept it,
Knowingly,
Peacefully.

MOTHERING

Thank you, mum,
for all your mothering,
For listening for hours,
For looking after us.
Although we have grown up,
We have not grown away.

FEELING

Feeling
Trapped, nowhere to
Turn, anxiety and
Sorrow growing from thoughts adrift
Breathe, peace.

TO BE HEARD

Slicing through loneliness,
A voice reaching through darkness,
Whispering in the night,
'I am here.'

Defeating the anguish,
A hand reaching through despair,
Listening in the moment,
'You are here.'

Needing solace and relief,
Souls reaching out to be heard,
Weeping in the void,
'They are here.'

Answering the cries,
Reaching out with humanity,
Holding broken pieces,
'We are here.'

ANNIVERSARY

Blustering winds,
Take memories to the hills,
Silver birches,
The only celebration.
Love did not last
beyond 'paper'.

TODAY'S NEWS

The illusion of compassion
Has left society
Now only delusion
and fear remain.

QUIET MOMENTS

In the quiet moments,
Let there be peace,
Not just an absence of war,
Or sound,
But a tranquillity of feelings,
Thoughts and reactions,
A deeper understanding,
Of our human condition,
Of the needs of others,
Of our own selves.
In those moments,
May we know,
Contentment,
And calm.

WELL SPOKEN

A chinwag, a chat,
How about that?
A talk that's sublime,
When we have the time,
A coffee, or tea?
Sounds good to me,
A time to share,
To show that we care,
Halving a problem,
Chewing the fat,
A witter, a twitter,
Let's get it off pat,
A prattle and prate,
Let's talk 'til it's late,
Let's gossip anew,
As that's what friends do!
Put the world to rights,
And sleep well at night,
Thank you for the years,
And your listening ears!

LIVING NIGHT

The stars sparkle in indigo pockets,
The moon whispers stories of peaceful sleep,
The birds are silent in their slumbering,
Foxes forage in darkened foliage,
Badgers emerge from their underground setts,
Trees stand guard, protecting smaller creatures,
From the sharp gaze of wise, feathered hunters,
The night has a busy life of its own.
People rest and renew strength in their homes,
Sleep brings respite from a long day's labour,
Dreams and ideas form like summer clouds,
Light and fresh, with hope for the coming days.
May the night be one that rejuvenates,
And brings happiness to all at sunrise.

KINDNESS

Sometimes, it feels like stepping along life's path takes courage;
take one step at a time.
There are days when we need to support another;
or we need similar support.
Speaking out is often difficult;
but it can help.
We all need more kindness in the world.

Forgiveness is hard;
but helps both parties.
A letter (or other communication)
can make someone's day.
You are creative and unique!
Treasure special memories;
may they bring comfort and joy.

NEED

When we are tired,
We cannot always see a way forward,
Don't forget to rest.

When we are hungry,
We cannot think and plan ahead,
Find nourishment and sustenance.

When our lights are dimmed by worry,
Share with another to pick out a path,
Worry itself achieves nothing.

When we are feeling down,
Reach out for company, do not lose hope,
Remember: you are not alone.

ACKNOWLEDGEMENTS

I'd like to thank Mark Davidson of Hedgehog Poetry Press for publishing my first pamphlet, 'Thoughts on Life'. I am delighted that this was the joint winner of the 'And I'm Feelin' Good -Trois' Competition in 2022.

Thank you to Liz Stirk for her beautiful cover illustration and over thirty years of friendship, you are a star!

Thank you to Melanie Broughton of 'Moment of Proof' copy editing for your invaluable support.

A great big thank you goes to Florrie Crass for her lovely quote and helping me to continue sharing my poetry.

A huge thank you to Ian Bland, for his kind words, quotation and advice about poetry work.

Thank you to my husband, Neil, for all your support and tech advice.

I have so many family members and friends to thank, there is not space to name you all, but 'Thank you!'